Soul Reflections

LINDA VILLEGAS BREMER

BALBOA.
PRESS

A DIVISION OF HAY HOUSE

Balboa Press books may be ordered through booksellers or by contacting:

Balboa Press
A Division of Hay House
1663 Liberty Drive
Bloomington, IN 47403
www.balboapress.com
1 (877) 407-4847

Because of the dynamic nature of the Internet, any web addresses or links contained in this book may have changed since publication and may no longer be valid. The views expressed in this work are solely those of the author and do not necessarily reflect the views of the publisher, and the publisher hereby disclaims any responsibility for them.

The author of this book does not dispense medical advice or prescribe the use of any technique as a form of treatment for physical, emotional, or medical problems without the advice of a physician, either directly or indirectly. The intent of the author is only to offer information of a general nature to help you in your quest for emotional and spiritual well-being. In the event you use any of the information in this book for yourself, which is your constitutional right, the author and the publisher assume no responsibility for your actions.

Any people depicted in stock imagery provided by Thinkstock are models, and such images are being used for illustrative purposes only.
Certain stock imagery © Thinkstock.

Printed in the USA.

ISBN: 978-1-5043-9558-8 (sc)
ISBN: 978-1-5043-9560-1 (hc)
ISBN: 978-1-5043-9559-5 (e)

Library of Congress Control Number: 2018901307

Balboa Press rev. date: 02/28/2018

Introduction

Welcome! Why have I written these tributes? I am convinced that each of us shows up with our special gifts – talents. I believe each day is the time to celebrate who we are – and honor others. I learned this from my parents – who demonstrated generosity, mysticism and spiritual connection – the Hispanic way, their own intimate way.

When I let go of expectations and simply accept another's life expression, I am delighted. Someone shared with me that the gifts of expectancy are bountiful – when I am open to possibility rather than to my brain's historical judgments. I love that.

Life is to be savored. Life is opportunity in action – potential waiting to be expressed. The light of discovery brings revelation. It's interesting to see my proficiencies in someone else or see in them that which I want to emulate.

I believe in this infinite Universe where anything is possible. When I meet someone, work with someone, take a class with someone – I endeavor to embrace their gifts with childlike wonder and curiosity.

We are each choosing. Creating. I am savoring this bountiful life. Join me.

Let us make this the time –

> ...for caring enough to lift a spirit – our spirit
> ...for taking a moment to appreciate our breath
> ...for being thankful for what we take for granted
> ...for connecting heart-to-heart with those close to us
> ...for helping someone else grow
> ...for growing into our highest self, for learning
> ...for doing more of what serves us, of what serves others.

I invite us to come together and expand our living life at another level of gratitude, abundance and joy!

Dedication

The raindrops splash heartily upon the welcoming soil –
  Boosting the emergent kernels of life to thrive.
The mother goose stands regally on the path –
  Safe-guarding the baby ducklings on their way across.
Loving parents serve with their souls in their hands –
  Providing sustenance to their offspring.
I am one with the magnificent flow of that considerate life energy.

Have you seen a baby in a father's arms – bubbling with delight?
The child feels safe. Feels cherished. Feels all is right with the world.
I am one with the awe-inspiring love of infinity in motion

How about a nursing female dog?
As each little puppy makes its entrance, its mother carefully tends to its
first needs – licking and cleaning her newborn to stimulate breathing
and to encourage nursing. She curves her body around them for
protection and warmth – hearts beating in unison.
I am one with the drive of the Universe to nurture heartwarming vitality.

For some animal fathers, "daddy duty" is a big deal.
Winter in Antarctica is bitterly cold. That's when a mother emperor
penguin lays her single egg. Then off she goes to the ocean to hunt for
food. Papa Penguin stays behind, balancing the egg on his feet and
keeping it warm under his belly feathers. He gathers with the other dads
as the wind howls. He can't let the egg touch the ice, or it will freeze.
I am one with the dance of Divine Intelligence – in harmony, in community.

In this moment in eternity, I am…

Mutuality   *Optimism*   *Magnificence*

Determination   *Abundance*   *Dependability*

I am devotion and accountability in action. I am.

Thank you, mom and dad! You inspired and encouraged. You loved.

Contents

"The magic of me came to be
    Quite naturally, you see.
        For I'm simply a …
            Reflection of …
                The love of you and me."

It's been quite a revelation to me to see myself in others' ways of being.
We are all one is easy to affirm.
Seeing the shimmering flashes of Spirit in others is also easy.
Seeing the same splendor in me, well, that's getting easier.
The radiant beams that are who I am chase away the shadows that attempt to mask my inheritance.
Thank you, God.

These expressions are inspired by the angels in my life, my friends—my fellow earth travelers.

My friend Joyce is an expert organizer.
Wherever she shows up, there seems to be a natural alignment in our cosmos.
Order. Rhythm. Life.

I stood on the boardwalk
    mesmerized by the waves as they ebbed and flowed—
        a miracle in action!
Turbulent green sheets of glass pounded in and pulsed out,
    edges unfurling in thick white ruffles.
The rhythm of life. Echoing the order in the universe.

My breath resonated in that same syncopation. In. Out. In. Out.
I felt that my entire body had been born with the innate knowing of
this reverent symphony.
My heart throbbed in time with this cadence.
Whish—om—whish—om.
These were the sounds as the waves crashed upon the shore. In. Out.
In. Out.

Order. Rhythm. Life.

The stars, the planets, the galaxies all vibrate in time with this holy
pacing.
How is it that I could ever doubt my divine nature, my talents for
organization and manifestation?
The leaves swaying in the breeze,
    the birds chirping in the trees,
        the sun setting in the sky,
            the clouds floating, passing by.

Joy in God's magnificent plan.
One with God's life-giving hand.
Yes to the universal syncopation.
Centered in divine order and demonstration.
Exuberant in my life's celebration!

I glow.
    I love.
        I prosper.
            I contribute.
                I am.

I took a class with Valerie.
What energy!

I am having a love affair with life, life in all its appearances.

The bustling of a teeming city.
    The opulence of a verdant valley.
        The vibrancy of the ocean.
            The majesty of a mountain range.
                The abundance of a rain forest.
                    The expansiveness of the desert.

I breathe in the essence of being.
I am filled with all that is eternal, for in this moment, I experience the miracle of the universe.

This miracle declares that:
    all that is, was, and that which will be are all imbued with holiness;
    all struggles are followed by triumph;
    all change leads to growth and renewal;
    all thanksgiving heralds joy;
    all hope sustains;
    all faith enlivens;
    all is in divine order.

In my love of the mortal and the immortal, I live in exultation.

I am
    Valiant as I eagerly welcome each day,
        Ardent as I support others in their fruition,
            Light as I dance the tango of the stars,
                Elegant as I show up in each moment,
                    Resourceful as I deal with the unanticipated,
                Insightful in my spiritual excursion,
                  Energetic as I master my lessons.

I am resilient.
    I accept my impermanence.
        I am on my soul's journey.
            I am a goddess in action.
I am love.

Marilyn and I are fellow faith travelers in the same sacred community.

She has been a passenger for quite a few decades on this blue bus we call Earth.

She inspires me with her love for learning and childlike view of all things here.

When I gaze into the sky, there is no east or west.

   We have created this artifact of directions so that we can physically
                                                   describe our world.

When the sun comes up in the morning and sets at night, there is no
clock.

   We invented this device so that we could regulate our schedules of
                                                   rest and activity.

When the days are followed by nights time and time again, there is
no calendar.

                      We fabricated the weeks and months so that we
                               could mark the passing of time.

Time and space are continuous, seamless, flowing across our grand
universe.

   So, what is age? A number.

I believe we concocted this notion because our temporal brains
needed a compass to track our journey on the planet. I can imagine
the very first persons to inhabit earth wanting to make sense of their
new home having to invent a language that had not existed. Amazing.

We have even imposed a gauge on trees by counting rings to
determine how long they've been alive.

   How long they've been alive.

What if we asked, "How have you lived?" instead of "How long have
you lived?"

What if, instead of age, we agreed on appraising the experiences that
have enlivened us?

What would happen if we eliminated words like *old, aged, elderly,
ancient*?

Could we be creative when we describe our aliveness?

How would we talk about those who arrived on the planet before we
did, such as our parents' parents?

I have lived with zeal. I have lived with joy.
I have lived through my personal adversity.
I have loved and both gained and lost.

I am living in the moment.
I am learning more every day.
I am surrounded by love—family, friends, community.
I am grateful for every step that has brought me here.
I am thriving more and more with every breath I take.
I am alive!

**Miracles. Abundance. Radiance. Inspiration.
Laughter. Yet to be. Now.**

The measure of time is man-made.
I am shaped by the spirit of all life.
I am God's beloved child.
I am beguiled by the magic of each new day.
I am.

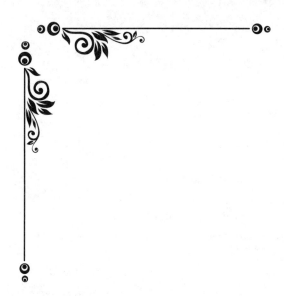

Robyn is a teacher.
Her sense of prosperity propelled me to dig deeper.

Like a river in motion,
like a planet spinning in space,
like a shoot finding its way through the earth's crust,
I am in the flow.

Like the clouds floating in air,
like the waves crashing on the rocks,
like the unfolding love in a child's optimism,
I am in the flow.

Yes, I am in the stream of universal good.
There is no beginning and no end—there is only the moment.
I am a parent, and I am a child. I am a teacher,
and I am a learner.
I love, and I am loved. I give, and I receive.

God is the origin of the prosperity in my life's garden. God is the
source of my wealth.
I am one with that wellspring of all that is.
I am whirling across the cosmos's vastness imbued with the
abundance of the universe.

In this oneness with God, I know I am
    Radiant in my expression, an
        Oasis for those in my presence,
            Blessed in my work, the
                Yin and the yang of completion, with
                    No limits on my prosperity.

I create channels for the whooshing power of plenty with every breath I take.
People around me honor me with their trust. I have faith in others. I am trustworthy.

I am courage and daring demonstrating.

I am instilled with God's potentiality, and I unleash it.

I am a work in progress. I am perfect, and all is in divine order.

Thank you, Spirit, for circulating all Your good in, around, and through me.

I release.

I am infinite. I am growth. I am creation. I am abundance.

And so it is.

Brenda.
A mom working hard to make ends meet.

The planets sprint in synchronicity across the vast expanse of our
   galaxy.

This rhythm of life vibrates through every speck of life and all matter.
   My breath refreshingly and soothingly flows in and out in
   accompaniment.

This spirit of all things working together for fulfillment
   brightens every step I take.

Life has brought many surprises—some more positive than others.

When I have faced challenges, I have done so with the courage of
Spirit in me.

Most important, I am grateful for the bounty of the wondrous
dreams that have manifested, my heart's desires come true.

   I exult in the wonder of my child.
      I rejoice in the blessings of sacred friendships.
         I appreciate the lessons of my master teachers.
         I bless the beauty of my world.
            I celebrate the generosity of the universe.

And so it is that I know I am God in action and that …

Bliss is my birthright.
   Radiance is my luster.
      Enthusiasm empowers me.
        Nurturing is my talent.
          Daring to thrive is my gift.
            Abundance is my birthright.

        I am creative.
        I am compassionate.
        I am confident.
        I am cherished.
        I am.

There are people dedicated to working with children who are living with physical challenges.
These aides heal with their touch, their hearts, and their love.
Kathie is one of these angels.
A manifestation of goodness in this world.

Goodness in the world.

The clouds caressing the sky.
The fog embracing the trees.
The sun soothing the earth.
The rain sprinkling love on parched places.

The inexhaustible charity of a caregiver.
The loving kindness in a child's kiss.
The unconditional love of a mother nursing her
infant.
The healing touch of a friend.

In this feeling of utter joy, I am filled with wonder that I am
surrounded by such generosity.

I tune in to our planet's healers whose reservoirs of goodwill are vast.
They support children in their struggle to overcome the entrapment of
their unresponsive bodies.

They are
    Kind in their actions,
        Ardent in their commitment,
            Trustworthy in all things,
                Heart-centered in their intentions,
                    Incandescent in their sharing,
                        Empathic in their love.

They see into the souls of those they serve—
  caring, meeting, respecting, finding common ground, giving these
  children what they need.

God's openhanded plan crafted opportunities for angels to walk
among us. Aren't we blessed?

They tend to those heroic children who remind us
    that the material is not who we are,
      that the physical limits in contrast to eternal life magnify the
      breadth of life.

    They inspire us as they are filled with hope in the
    next day.
    They serve us by demonstrating that not all challenges
    defeat.
    They lead us in finding our way from victim to victor.

I am a child of God.
I am alive.
I am learning.
I am teaching.
I am grateful.
I am.

Stephen is a community leader, a mayor.
He contributes so that my quality of life is enhanced.
He is selfless.

Ants everywhere, scurrying around, following an inner knowing of the job they are destined to perform, laboring for the good of the many.

Geese flying in formation, soaring across the sky, taking turns relieving the lead bird and taking care of the weak, laboring for the good of the many.

A whale pod, frolicking in the sea, whirling underneath the waves, caring for each other, protecting the young, laboring for the good of the many.

A lion's pride—males and females roving the savannah grasslands—working together, searching for shade and food to ensure their progeny survive, laboring for the good of the many.

And so it is that many of our fellow earthly trekkers choose to serve with courage and integrity so that their neighbors and those who are vulnerable have someone who advocates for them, laboring for the good of the many.

This is the stuff of life—sustaining, celebrating, restoring, witnessing.

Who are these people?
    Some teach, some heal, some listen, some minister, some run for office,
        courageous in placing their convictions on the line.
    They are willing to go way past good enough, past the status quo.
    They are grounded in principle and lead by pursuing an exceptional, inspired vision of our duty to good.
    They weave a dynamic and vital fabric of goodwill.
    They appreciate points of view disguised as challenges that bring magnificent potential to life.

We are here, together in time, creating this slice of history
—our space, our time, our texture of reality.

Substance is my hallmark.
Trust is my mantle.
Engagement and inclusion of others' perspectives are my
guides.
Potential is a beacon that beckons.
Honesty is in my being.
Excellence is my contribution.
Namaste.

I am open.
I am receptive.
I am accepting.

I am ONE with all that is.

I took a class called "A Year to Live."
Our leader on this spiritual expedition was Patty.
A master guide.

There is a divine well of wisdom within me. This well is infinite.
It has no beginning, and it has no end. It is endless, unbounded,
unlimited. It is God.
This "divine well" in me is part of our grand spirituality—the
divinity of the Infinite.

It is from this wellspring that thoughts and words arise. I love words!
I revel in sliding the letters around a virtual lever and reconfiguring a
new word.

I believe in the power of words.
More important, I believe in the magic of the thoughts from which
those words vault.

As a thought germinates in my brain, it springs from nothingness.
Isn't that amazing?
That means I have the power to breed whatever notions I choose.
When I opt for rapture and happiness, I can shellac the gem that is
my soul with a vibrancy that will stimulate my heaven on earth.

Many words shimmer with power.
Words such as aspiration, beacon, celebration, divinity,
enlightenment, flight, glow, harmony, intimacy, joy, kindness, love,
mystery, nourishment, opulence, peace, quiescence, radiance, spark,
triumph, unity, vitality, wonder, x-citement, youth, zest.

I aspire to be a beacon celebrating divinity and enlightenment—
elements of my birthright.
My soul takes flight as I bask in the glow and harmony of the
intimacy of the Universe's life light.
Joy, kindness, and love exalt the mystery that nourishes the opulence
of my inner sight.

Peace and quiescence pair up to balance radiance and spark—the gifts of spiritual delight.
I am triumphant. I am in unity with Divine Spirit. I am a vital Being affirming wonder and might.
The X-citement of youth and the zest of the innocent are within my reach. They are my sacred right.

My teachers—guides, sorcerers, wizards—have taught me the magic of words,
        the seeds of manifestation.
I am grateful for those spirits in my life who have nurtured me
into spelunking the depths of my soul so that I may recognize my
Universal Source.
My spiritual teachers remind me that I am one with all that is.

They are:
Patient in my unfoldment in my own time;
    Accepting in my journey that is sometimes resistant to change, to
        the mystery of growth;
        Trusting in that celestial essence that is who I am;
            Triumphant in my discovery of Faith;
                Yearning for my next step, in love.

And again and again, they join with me so that I may accept the
waters of the Fountain of eternal life—infinite knowing.

> I am a teacher.
> I am a student of life.
> I am blissful.
> I am.

Sharon is a Religious Science Practitioner, a facilitator, a teacher.
She nurtures.
As a mom, letting go is delicate.

Mother of all that is, you are the Source of Life, of expression, of learning, of being.
You are timeless, always here.
You are the vessel that transplants a child across the oceans of essence and manifestation.

You are the fertile ground awaiting the seed of the physical plane so that Spirit can be born demonstrating into form.

I, too, am a mother. Before the embryo came to life in my womb, I was once an embryo. And before my origin expressed, my mother was there ready for my appearance. And so are the threads of our lives' fabric woven, with no beginning and no end, with no regard for space and time, an infinite circle of love.

Mother of all that is, I know that I am channeling life's creative force. There is only One.

In this Oneness, I am the magic of this eternal moment.
I release all ideas of separation. My child and I are One.
No matter the false impression of having space
between us, the Universe sees only One.

I am …
Sparkling …
Heavenly …
Ardent …
Replenished …
Open …
Nurturing.

My child is always with me; I am always with my child.
I love unconditionally.
I have faith in my child's choices. I nurture to fruition and no more.
I let go.
Even when our souls leave this enchanted planet, we are always One.
In the space of my heartbeat, I know that any corporeal chasm is only an illusion.

Mother of all things, I joyfully accept my child's independence, my child's decisions.

I exult in the totality of the love I feel.

I vibrate with the resonance of shared souls.

I am whole.
I am One.
I release.
I am.

There are times when I feel less confident than other times.
Why?
I am always steeped in God's love.
What gives?
Susan struggled with being confident.
She opened new pathways to rediscovering my soul's poise.

Anytime I listen to children at play, I hear their spontaneity.
I feel their creativity. I sense their confidence. They know that they
know.

Isn't it fantastic how they intuit their grandeur?
They are creative without deep thinking. They instinctively know how
to have fun.

It is easy to realize that just as a flower knows how to bloom,
just as a butterfly knows how to metamorphose,
just as a cloud knows how to rain,
and just as my blood knows how to nourish my cells,
I too know that my life's expression is all that it must be.

I know this for I am One with You, the fountain
of life, of the cosmos, of all …

It is apparent to me that at times I paid
attention to others' judgments of me.

It is crystal clear to me that I am magic!

I am …
Sovereignty expressing …
Uniqueness come to life …
Success manifested …
Ambition in motion …
Newborn in the moment.

Thank you, God, for this confidence that is my birthright.
There is no right, no wrong; no tight, no loose;
no strong, no weak; no above, no below.
There is only Being—along this magnificent earthly journey.

In each moment, I am divine.
In each moment, I am wondrous.
In each moment, I can do anything.

Thank you! Thank you! Thank you!

I am thrilled to recognize the confident person I have always been
and always will be,
For I am a star in the Universe of galaxies.

I am evolving in each moment.

And so it is.

Chuck is a pal who is an auditor.
Playing with numbers is his game.
The synchronization of the Universe resides in his mathematics.

The waves brush the sands on the shore with the lulling rhythm of
the ocean's soul.

The rain that taps on my windowpane feels like the heartbeat of the
Universe.

The rustling of the leaves in the trees soothes me to my core.

My breathing—soft as a feather's kiss—restores me,

and I can simply be.

This calm, peace, and harmony emanate from You, the Source of all
that is.

You, God, are the wellspring of the serenity that every cell in my
body relaxes into.

My consciousness is filled with …
Contentment,
Harmony,
Unity,
Calm,
Kindness.

For I realize that I am One with the Universal life force,
in exactly the same way that a wave on the sea is integral to the
brine essence.

I am grateful for every opportunity in space-time to release anxiety
and concern.

I let go of doubt.

I eliminate fear and anger.

Each moment, I experience more and more peacefulness.

My cup runneth over.
It expands ever more as I allow further tranquility and honesty into my day's expression.

Dear God, my body is permeated with Your Love and perfect health. In this quiet space, I know that I am healed of any imbalance in my bodysuit and in Mind.

Thank you for all that I can see in my existence and all that is unseen that blesses me.

I am calm.

I am peace.

I am stillness.

I am grateful.

I have goddesses around me.
There is mutual adoration in infinite supply.

Diane blesses me.
She teaches how to let go of image.

The earth spins on its axis, transporting me among the stars.
    I am an astral invention.
        I am stellar.

The Universal life source fuels every bit of energy that is and is yet to be.
    I am love in action.
        I am celestial.

The fountain of possibilities is the center from which 'all that is' emanates.
    I am filled with Light.
        I am creation.

I rejoice! For I am One with this miracle of all substance.

I am …
    Divine spark,
        Invitation,
            Acceptance,
                Nobility,
                    Eternity.

I accept my genuineness. I let go of false image.

I am illumination. I release all doubt.

Thank you, God.

In You, I am free to express in any form.

The vastness of my reach is astounding in its unboundedness.

I appreciate the gifts of freedom and enlightenment.

I am wise and prosperous, and I accept others. I accept me.

With every glimmer of luminosity in the present moment, I am true—faithful to my soul.

These gifts and all the reverence in the universal storehouse of talents are mine.

I revel in my Joy!

And so it is.

I have heard it said that worrying is a futile exercise. I believe it.
Furthermore, I know that doubt is its sibling. It too is a thief.
It is such a gift to become more aware of the converse of these
illusions.
My pal Judy is a mirror for me.

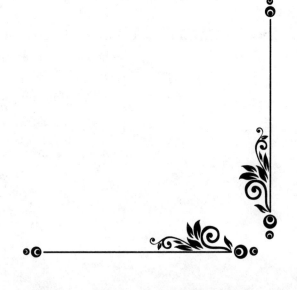

We are born imbued with Faith.

Faith grows in spite of disappointments.

Faith is ever-present regardless of conditions.

I say, Yes, Yes and Yes!

God, I recognize that You are the Source of all that is.
You are the Ultimate embodiment of Faith.

The sun rises in the morning.
The moon and the stars shine at night.
The waves on the ocean soothingly sweep the shore.
The sky's mantle high above holds us close in the day's light.

These miracles abound.
I know not how or why; all I know is that they are the heartthrob of
the Universe,
steadfast, reliable, and judgment-free.

I too am a marvel … a magical twinkle … a magnificent ember … a
miracle of life …

As I detach and look impartially at my past, I see choices.
Choices that were wise and choices that were ill-considered.

God, You are always with me, spurring me on to greatness in spite of appearances.

"Thy will is done in me this day and every day."

My faith sustains me.

In this Oneness with all that is—with You, the Universal Source—I find that I am …

    Jewels dazzling with my light.

        Uplifting with my trust,

            Delighting in my love, I say

                Yes! To Life. I must!

                    What splendor!

                    What ecstasy!

                    What sanctity!

                    I give thanks!

JR.
What a Spirit.
She held judgment and anger up to the light.

The gift of forgiveness is ever "on tap."

I declare my passion. Life's adoration of me is thrilling.
I accept the gifts Faith brings.
I manifest an easy, loving Life's dance.
I am in a pleasurable state.

Here's to releasing into my divine truth.
    I deserve and accept joy, energy, and health.
        I am complete in God.
           I am.

I breathe in and feel God's love.
    I exhale and feel God's life.
I scan my world and see God's gifts.
    I feel my heartbeat, and I forgive.

As I tread upon this magical planet, I am in touch with the vibrancy of all-being.

Though there may be a drought, the trees are not resentful.
Though the snow blankets the bloom,
    The rose will sleep and awaken peacefully in the spring.
All around me—for situations that I judge as harsh—
    Nature says, "All is in divine order." Spirit renews.

God, I recognize that this handiwork on
earth comes directly from You.
You who manifested the stars, the moons, and
the galaxies also manifested me.
We are all One. We are the Universe.

In this Oneness, I accept that I am …

Joyful!   Resilient!
Jaunty!   Rare!
Jubilant!   Resplendent!

In the majesty of my soul ablaze with love and bliss, I know that I am
forgiving the smallest and the largest of hurts. I know for certain that
the trickery of fear and resentment is superfluous. I let go.
I recognize that these transgressions stem from others' fears and
illusions.

At times, others may disappoint for not living up to my image of
them.
     I am free. I let go of expectations. I release judgment.
     I immerse myself in love

With each step I take on my mortal adventure, I immerse myself in a
pool of forgiveness.
     The clear water washes any residue of
     disappointment from my essence.

I am whole. I am serene. I am!
I am free to be me and let others be.

There are Spirits among us who are more in touch with their psychic talents than most.
They serve to show us that we are all here with the same access to the storehouse of good.

Lacey teaches and inspires.

Throughout the fabric of time and space, the Universe unfurls its
mysteries.
    I clearly feel the solid ground under my feet.
        The majestic blue dome I call a sky surrounds me.

In the ether of my essence, I am in touch with angels and guides.
    In my person, I channel healing energies.
        I am certain, sure, and confident that I am cherished, loved,
            adored.

God, You are the Source of all that is—of all that I see and all that I
cannot even imagine.

                You are generous in Your gifts. You provide
                    a Universe of super-possibilities.

I am One with You …
    Just as the raindrop that falls on the ocean is one with that
mighty sea.

My inheritance of infinite splendor and magnificence heals my heart
of any illusory pain.
My heart is the nucleus of emotional life.
My deepest and sincerest feelings reside here.
My empathy for reviving souls is great!
I heal any heartache through my faith in Spirit.

In my divinity, I know I am expressing …
Love,
Authenticity,
Creation,
Energy, and I say
Yes! To the goddess in me!

Bathed in the radiance of gratitude,
I accept that as You, as Spirit, as God, I am able to allow others to feel their hurts, their pain, their grief, and I am whole.

I let go.
I forgive.
I embrace joy.
I am zest-full.

And so it is.

Coaching a group of kids is more than a talent;
it's a gift of educing confidence and another's gifts.

Dave is one of those special cherubs.

He is a husband, a dad, a trainer, a therapist, and a businessman.

I have so much fun when I see my children at play!
When my team wins, every cell in my body pounds with
excitement.
Having a growing business is way cool!
And being in love is the grandest wonder of all!

The magnificence of the Universe surrounds me in each moment.
The fascinating mechanism that is the body is the arena in which I
perform.
I heal. I create well-being.

I thrive on that fundamental healing energy that flows effortlessly
through me.
I rejoice in my ability to restore others to health.
My physical condition is perfect through Your grace.
I am whole. I am healed.

I do all this in my Oneness with Spirit.
Thank you, God.

For, as you, I am …
Daring in passion,
Achieving in life,
Vibrating in the cosmos,
Exuberant in my playfulness.

God, I accept perfect health.
I accept prosperity.
I accept wisdom.
I tell the truth.

I know that all these gifts and more are my divine birthright.
I open the windows of possibility, and I accept your abundance.
And so it is.

If we are to measure a time span in years, Toy is well on her way to one hundred.
She still takes classes.
She shows up with energy and verve.
She is a pathfinder.

Through the passage of time, the centuries flow one into another ...
The traditions travel across generations ...
My ancestors are my genesis.

God, I recognize that You are the Source of all that is.
You are the fountainhead of existence.

I am One with You, just as ...
the breath I release becomes the atmosphere ...
the wave that crests becomes ocean,
the dew that fortifies is infused into the bloom,
and the fuel that motorizes becomes motion.

God, in this sense of connection, I accept
Truth,
Order,
You!
Talent,
Openness,
You!

Thank you for my teachers, my friends, and my children.
I am grateful for the learning that transforms me.
I am free to be me.
I release any stories of pain and injustice.
I forgive, and I move on to paradise.

I am love.
I am whole.
I am strong.
I endure.
I thrive.

Sometimes I grouse. I whine.

When I'm sick, I think my trifle of an illness is overwhelming.

When something doesn't go my way, I can slip into singing a "poor me" ballad.

When I find myself struggling, it's easy to ask, "Why me?"

And then I think of my friend Luther.

Bound to a wheelchair and vibrantly engaged in life.

Thank you for inspiring me to go beyond form.

Once upon a time, when the Universe of potential was my home, I
existed as God-Spirit.
Then I took on a form, as an actor dons a character, and I was born
here on earth.
My play is splendid. My theater—a stage of learning and challenge!
I am here to teach.

The Universe—that circle of eternal manifestation is expressing
as me ...
    Loving,
       Unique and unlimited,
          Triumphant,
             Healing,
                Enlightened, and
                    Revealing.

The islands on the planet's surface appear to be totally independent.
In reality, they originate from the same earth's core. They are one
formation.

You, God, are the master artist who designed each
handiwork as a specific one-of-a-kind-beauty.
An atoll never compares itself to another island.
A frozen isle does not resent the tropical zone.
Nature cries out in exultation for the magic, the mystery,
the magnificence that is Spirit articulating.

I am One with You. This is my birthright, the only reason I exist.
I am invincible.
Wherever I go, I provoke those around me
to live with verve and curiosity.
Thank you, God.
I accept the gifts of intelligence, wisdom, and forgiveness.
Here's to life!

I release all that does not evolve me.
   Any limitations are illusory, for in God, I am almighty.

I am dazzling. I am holy. I am light. I am promise. I am success. I am timeless. I am life.
I inspire!

There is someone I am close to who sometimes surprises me.
The more I get to know her, the more I appreciate her.
I am that someone.
I love Linda more each day.

There is no space. There is no time. There is only God.

There is …
>   abundance, beauty, choice, dance, expectancy …
>   faith, genius, heart, imagination, justice …
>   kinship, laughter, mind, nature, opportunity …
>   praise, quiet, radiance, supply, treasure …
>   unconditional love, vision, wholeness, xenia, *yatra*,
>   zeal …
>   and so much more!

As I look around me, I see the tangible aspects of our galaxy, a mass of stardust spinning through the millennia toward somewhere we cannot fathom.
This whirling amalgam of astrophysical stuff appears to be a speck in an infinite Universe.

Modern quantum mechanics is raising the possibility of this universe nudging other universes.
Our thoughts of reality are as primitive as the notion that the world was flat.

Science now says that it is entirely possible that I am like a hologram come to life in this realm, an outward expression of a greater essence. For now, instead of three dimensions and time, mathematics declares there are ten or eleven dimensions.

And what does science postulate about time?
There is no scientific basis for temporal judgments as we know them.

In this paradoxical wonder of certain uncertainty,
    I am grounded in my Oneness with Spirit.

I accept the truth about God as the Source of my supply.
I give thanks for powerful Law that demonstrates as me in each
moment.

I am ...
Laughter ...
Innovation ...
Newness ...
Divinity ...
At-one-ment ...

Dearest, God, I embody gratitude. I am compassion in action. I am.

Living in the moment, for the moment.
I met Steve in a workshop.

He is a rascal! Irreverent, natural, and authentic.

Spontaneous!
Tenacious!
Eager!
Vivid!
Evolving!

Life is filled with expressions of natural gusto—of purpose—of integrity.

A newborn puppy.
A fluttering hummingbird.
A tree-climbing squirrel.
A buzzing bumblebee.

I know Spirit as that ingenious life-giving Source.

I am one with that Divine Mind.
I have a deep knowing that I am here to serve.
I am here to support those around me!
I am here to celebrate life!
I am here to channel the planetary imperative for growth!

Right here, right now …

I choose love.
I choose wisdom.

I choose curiosity.
I choose abundance.

I choose wholeness.
I choose beauty.

What magnificent potential!
In this physical bodysuit, I revel in my providence.
    I know I am divinity expressing.

I am so very grateful.

    This is my big- 'T' Truth.

I am courage.
I am freedom.
I am joy.
I am prosperity.
I am.

Every time a musician is on stage, I instantly feel creative energy buzzing in and around me.

I so appreciate Scott—a technical guru, a friend, a passionate guitarist.

The birds were singing …
 The wind was whistling …
  The water fountain was gurgling …
  The leaves were murmuring …
As I walked toward the garden, I was touched by the harmony of
nature.
Listening to a bird's song, I was filled with wonder.
 The soft wind, in accompaniment, amplified the melody.
  What miracles!
   Right here! Right now!

I see how the melodious majesty of life led to that first person's
 manifestation of music!
 Who invented music? Who was that first person who sang?
  What was the first instrument? A percussion device?

   Originality! Inspiration! Ingenuity!
   Living the creative process …
   The ability to make music,
   invent new things, think of new ideas …

A flute that is forty thousand years old. An elephant skin drum that is
thirty-seven thousand years old.
Pan pipes imagined to be thirty thousand years old. Stringed
instruments over a thousand years old.
All devices fashioned from a spiritual knowing that music soothes …
enlivens … caresses …

 Sitting there, playing with my band, I started swaying in my chair.
  My feet tapped out the rhythm.
  My heart filled with emotion.

A **S**park of magic floated in the air.

A **C**onsecrating vibration resonated in that holy space.

The **O**pportunity to experience unconditional love evolved.

Thriving in joy became effortless.

A **T**ransformation of spirituality lifted each soul.

What a remarkable gift!

Creating music. Sharing music. Appreciating music.

Reminding me of that inventive nature of Divine Mind.

Reminding me that life is a symphony.

In reality, every moment gives me an opportunity to live with a creative spirit.

I take time to remember that, ultimately, my LIFE is my greatest work of art.

Each moment gives me another chance to most fully embody my highest ideals and rock it.

I am Originality! I am Inspiration! I am Ingenuity!

I am Gentleness! I am Gratitude!

I am a powerful, self-aware person who lives without fear.

I am Spirit expressing.

I am!

Spiritual Guides. Ministers. Priests. Rabbis. Imams. And more …

They bless.

Systematically Facilitating Fulfillment through the Divine Creative
Process …
That's what I do!

Can you feel it?
God's love flowing through you as you!
God's love flowing through me as me!
God's love flowing through us as us!

What a gift!
I am willing to be a messenger for Good.

Sometimes I hear someone talk about "an ordinary existence."
Really?
The human design is a divine blueprint!
My sacred essence is at the core of this physical form.
Sublime intelligence is showing up as me! As you!
The wisdom of creation as my holy birthright fills me.

I believe in the immeasurable intelligence that hatched all that is,
was, and will be.
I believe I am a catalyst for the rebirth, the evolution, of a higher self.

I am passionate about possibility.
My work promotes a healing pattern for all the beings I touch, reach.

Who am I?
I am a child of God … a child awakened to the cosmic mind, the
supreme beloved.

My gifts are these and more ...
　　I am **R**esplendence.
　　I am **O**ptimism.
　　I am a **B**eacon for Faith.
　　I am **E**ternal.
　　I am **R**evelation.
　　I am **T**riumph.

I am like a seed—taking root, blooming, spreading offshoots of
enthusiasm and happiness.

I am like the wind—softly rushing, wafting, weaving through all of
life with whispers of reverence.

I am like the rain—steadily sprinkling, revitalizing, inspiring the
creative process inherent in life.

　　I am grateful.
　　　I am love.

　　　I am.

Love!

Love!

Love!

Everywhere! In everyone!

A while ago, I was walking through a nature trail, in awe of the wonder of the majestic trees.

Some had their arms spread wide open, relishing the sun.

Some were lying on the ground, nurturing new saplings.

Some had been broken in two, honoring their rooted sacred space.

I was filled with a sense of wonder and deep love for the offerings of the Universe.

Driving to visit a friend, I couldn't help but be spellbound by the marvels unfolding before me.

An expansive, glorious sky ...

Clouds of fog embracing the landscape ...

Emerald vegetation painting divinity ...

I was filled with love and reverence for God as all things seen and unseen.

Riding the train, I hear friends greeting friends. I see a father caring for a child.

I notice a couple snuggling and touching fondly.

Love! Love for all of life! Love for one another! Love for the sake of love! The ancient Greeks used four expressions to speak of love—agape, *phileo*, *storge*, and eros.

Love abounds!

Agape. Unconditional "God" love—an unconditional love for all that is, that sees beyond the outer surface and accepts, regardless of flaws or shortcomings. I love because of who I am.

Phileo. Friend bond—affectionate, warm, and tender platonic love— to be a friend, have affection. I love because of who you are.

Storge. Empathy bond—love for family members, friends, pets, and companions or colleagues. It can help underpin compassion, passionate love, and friendship. It's committed, sacrificial. I forgive because I love.

Eros. Erotic bond—passionate and intense love that arouses romantic, emotional, and sexual feelings. Eros (or being in love) is in itself an indifferent, neutral force. I love because I feel.

I breathe in all Love.
   I breathe in …
      connection, appreciation, beauty, closeness …
   I breathe in …
      joy, encouragement, kindness, gusto …
   I breathe in …
      tenderness, romance, passion, intimacy …
   I breathe in
      camaraderie, goodwill, harmony, nature …

I know God as love expressing in me.
I open my heart, mind, and soul to receiving love.
I am allowing and welcoming love!
I live and breathe that one life of love and gratitude.
I am **l**ove, **i**nspiration, **n**irvana, **d**evotion, **a**cceptance.
                  I love!

What about life?
    What about eternity?
        What about renewal?

My pal Linda motivates.

A spark flies off a burning log …
A shooting star streaks across the sky …
Lightning flashes abruptly, seemingly from nowhere …

Is that how the breath, the form of life comes to be?
In that place where everything resides and nothing exists, where all is form-less,
divine sparks ignite and launch
into the journey to the land of the formed.
Abracadabra! And a baby is born. What magic!

A master once asked, "When were you born?"
After I shared my birthday, he said, "Really? Did you exist before that day?"
"Yes, I was in my mother's body."
"And how did you come to be a fetus before germinating? Do you think that the matter that became you was there before then? And what about that which engendered your parents? Before the Universe even knew you in this form?"

Mysteries. Life ostensibly from nothing—yet spawned from Divine Source.

Once upon this earth, how is it that we are here with a clean slate for a memory?
What will it take to remember that the realm of the form-less is all that is?
And so what do we truly know about life? About death?
A dictionary defines death as "the ending of all fundamental functions or processes in an organism or cell."

How appropriate. It does not speak to non-existence, but rather it alludes to the possibility of transformation.

Miracles!

Luminosity and Love ...
    Imagination and Intention ...
        Nascence and Nurturing ...
            Desire and Demonstration ...
                Abundance and Appreciation ...

I am magic!
    I am a mystery!
        I am a miracle!
            I am the expectancy of the Universe personified.
            I am fully living my life's purpose.
                I teach. I heal. I inspire.

When I go to a crafts fair, I am overcome by all the ingenuity.
I get to see my commonplace world in new ways.

Lin is a wise, resourceful connector.

Did you see that sky painted in coral, gold, and turquoise?
    A magnificent sunset!

    How about those ants scurrying around, bringing food home?
        A vibrant community!

A meadow in spring splashed with living color?
    A stunning field of flowers!

    A sapphire dome pierced with shimmering diamonds?
        An amazing night sky!

I feel the creative process bursting forth in me and all around me.
Even when I close my eyes, I am transported into the infinite.

This inspired determination flows through me in miraculous ways.

I am pulsating with inventive zing and vitality.
I am oozing ingenuity from every pore.
I am vibrating with nascent handiwork.
I am imbued with Spirit's artistic grace.
I am seen as the divine masterpiece that I am.

Limitless creation …
    Intention that is unbounded …
        Newness, inexhaustible …

So here I sit, breathing in my good …
    Blessed.
        Wise.
           Nurtured.
           Radiant.

Gratitude is expressing as me!

I co-create.
I fashion.
I craft.
I originate.

In Lea's presence, I feel light, affection, and verve.

She launches herself in love.
　　Wow!

I breathe in and feel God's love.
I exhale and feel God's life.
I scan my world and see God's gifts.
I feel my heartbeat, and my spirit lifts.

As I trod upon this magical planet, I am in touch with the vibrancy
of all-being.
Though there may be a drought, the trees endure.
Though the snow blankets the bloom, the rose sleeps,
    awakening peacefully in the spring.
All around me, for situations that I may judge as harsh,
    nature says, "All is in divine order."
    Spirit renews.

God, I recognize that this handiwork on
earth comes directly from You.
You who manifested the stars, the moons, and
the galaxies also manifested me.
We are all One. We are the Universe.

In this Oneness, I accept that …
I am **Light!**
I am **Elation!**
I am **Abundance!**

In the majesty of my soul ablaze with love and bliss …
I am open,
I am kind,
I am happy!

I let go.
I am grateful. I am free. I let go of expectations. I release judgment.
I throw myself at God! I fling myself at Love!
With each step of my mortal adventure, I immerse myself in a pool of understanding.
The clear water washes any residue of unfulfilled expectations from my essence.

I am whole. I am serene. I am!
I show up in my divinity.
I am free to be me and let others be.

What is abundance?
　　What is prosperity?
　　　　What is my measure?

With June, I had an opportunity to explore this and more ...
　　The flow of the breath of life.

Nature …
I witness the phenomena of the physical world …
　　I start with our planet, and soon I am transported across the
　　　　Universe.

As I look around, I am enfolded by miracles!
　　Quadrillions of grains of sand …
　　　　Billions of birds …
　　　　　　Trillions of ants …
　　　　　　　　Billions of trees …

I am in awe of the majesty that is my world. It is magical! It is
teeming with sacred mysticism.

I breathe in and out, and I ask, "Who is guiding the breathing?"
My blood circulates in my body, and I ask, "Who is guiding those
cells?"
There is a sweet engagement in all of life, in all of the cosmos.
All I know is that the energy that propels the stars is the same energy
pulsing as me.
The divine Source of all that is and ever will be I know as *my* Source.
I am one with Divine Mind.

And as I embody that notion—that Truth—my faith gets stronger.

I stand here with open arms, an open mind, a wide-open soul,
ready, willing, and available for more of God's good to flow
effortlessly through me, as me.

The lavishness all around stems from that same Divine Creative Spirit showing up as me.

The **J**oyous largesse of nature ...
　　The **U**nconditional compassion of the Universe ...
　　　　The **N**ew creations abounding ...
　　　　　　The **E**xuberant expressions of circulation, movement ...

All a divine expression—just as I am.

I accept this prosperity as my celestial inheritance.
　　I accept the abundance that is naturally mine.
　　　　I choose infinite, holy bounty.
　　　　　　I choose ease.
　　　　　　I choose being in the flow.

And I am grateful.
　　I am happy.
　　　　I am kindness.
　　　　　　I am creative.
　　　　　　　　I am unlimited.
　　　　　　　　I am.

Cynthia is a high achiever, a magnificent backer, a contributor.

I am struck by her audacity and devotion.

When I am with her, I am all smiles.

What am I here to do?
What am I here to be?

Powerful, empowering questions.

My life is filled with miracles!
This journey has taken me places I had not contemplated.
Often, I have walked unconsciously, as many have.

Where do I go from here?
How do I find my path?
Why?

I'm awake!
I know I am choosing.

There are times when my expanding awareness surprises me.
I discover "me's" that are a revelation.
I say to myself, "Wow! What a trip! That's who I am at times. Isn't it interesting?"
I am thrilled that I can do this neutrally, with curiosity.
It's not about right or wrong. It just is.
And I can choose again.
What delight!

I am God's divine child. I am limitless. In each moment, I am
growing into the best me yet!
I'm blessed by the people around me—learning lessons and
celebrating in each moment.

I know that ...

I am   Cherishing every breath I take, every friend I make.

I am   a Yowza kind of person—living with verve and
enthusiasm.

I am   Nifty, ingenious, clever, resourceful, creative, and
MORE!

I am   Tantalizing. This means I am enticing and
tormenting, teasing and provoking.

I am   like so Honest I can be annoying. And in a good way.

I am   Infinite—part of this beautiful never-ending sacred
circle of creation.

I am   Audacious. And I love it!

I accept myself exactly as I am.

People in my life have come to nourish, support.
    How blissful.
Susan is a generous, compassionate Soul.
She is a shaman, a healer.

Love around.

    Love within.

        Love in all that is.

I sit here in the comfort of solitude, contemplating the mysteries of the Universe.

I was born in this spinning, unanchored mass of stardust we call Earth.

When our cosmic blue bus is viewed from afar, it is truly a "blue dot" in the galactic canvas.

It shares the planetary space with other microscopic specks.

It is unfolding into eternity.

As am I.

All the energy in the Universe came to be in a single burst of life-creating power.

All that is, all that was, all that will be emerges from that sole surge of energy.

It's amazing. Somehow, I bought a ticket for this magic carpet ride.

My life is filled with material wonders *and* with the beauty of the mystical, spiritual gifts—

    love, generosity, wisdom, compassion, zeal, and more.

With each new day, I come across new revelations that lead me closer to my Divine Source. God!

It is easy to see that since the force flowing through all creation is flowing through me,

    I am revered. I am a unique expression. I am a miracle.

Sacred journey …
   Understanding heart …
      Sparkling discoveries …
         Adoring energy …
            Noble creations …
I accept my good with an open heart, a receptive mind, a willing soul.
I am grateful.
I am blessed.
I am complete.
I am worthy.
Wizardry is my way of life.

Bountiful, thriving spirits.
They are all around me.

Buffie is all this and more.

Manifestations.
    Miracles.
        Marvels.
I know I am the creator of my results.
As I take in this Truth, I appreciate that I am the conductor of
Universal energy.
Hallowed. Consecrated. Sanctified.
The Universe is biased in my favor.
I realize my fondest desires.
I listen to my heart and my soul.
I thrive in the lushness that is my earthly animation.
Whatever thought I think, I actualize.
This is way beyond survival; this is Godliness.
This is blooming, expanding, and finding the gift in the promise.
Conjuring is my feisty, Spirit-filled genius.

I am **B**lessed.
    I am **U**niversal.
        I am **F**ulfilled.
            I am **F**lourishing.
                I am **I**maginative.
                I am **E**vocative.

I wholeheartedly receive the bounty of the Universe.
I am so very grateful.
God's light is shining through me, as me.
I release this affirmation into that Divine Law that supports me.
I know this is so.
And it's about more than just me!
My fellow earth trekkers and I are clones reveling in this certainty of
creation.
I am ONE with my sacrosanct clan—with all that is.
I am magnificent.
I am glorious.

Family is special.
    Friends are delight.

Sue serves those in her sacred circle.
    She counsels. She blesses.

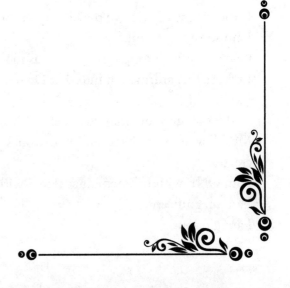

Sweet, sweet Spirit.

I have heard Your song from the beginning of the beginning.

It fills my soul with purpose and joy!

I know who I am! I know why I am here!

I am a divine essence, a mystic. I am here to honor my fellow beings.

What a delightful feeling!

I share my gifts, and souls reclaim their personal sovereignty, their authority.

They are empowered to open the windows of their opportunity consciousness.

    They transform from victims to victors.

I co-create in partnership with You, Divine Mind.

I am so grateful for my talents. I have multiplied that which You bestowed on me.

As I ponder the mysteries of universes upon universes, I am struck by the majesty of my life.

Whatever I imagine, I make happen.

I have thoughts to think, dreams to weave, and seeds to sow. I know *everything* is possible.

I am …

    Sensational …

        Unique …

            Eternal …

I am grateful for my birth family and their love.

I am grateful for my spiritual family and their inspiration.

I am cherishing and cherished.

I am teaching and learning.

I am connecting and bonded.

I make a difference.

I grow, and my highest good comes to me in ease.

I am "on fire" with my aspiration to heal.

I am alive!!!

Selena is a being so rich with many divine gifts.
She is a healer of lost hearts.

She has assisted souls who find the streets as domiciles.
    She has painted portraits just because.
        She has been a magnet for community donations.

I am in awe.

Oh, holy of holies!
I am blessed.
The Universe is blessed *and* blessing.
I look around me, and I see healing energy pulsing in all that is.
I am Divine Mind expressing.
I am One with all.
Zeal, enthusiasm, and imagination urge me on.
I am grounded in the knowing and the faith of all that is mine to do.

Yes!
I am participating fully with the souls that fill my circle of life.
Devotion. Adoration. Passion.
     This is who I am.
I am certain that Infinity has no beginning and no end.
I too am Immortal.
In this span of my existence, my heart is overflowing with love for my fellow earth travelers.
I see my journey as triumphant.
All that I need, I have.
I channel God's good, and it flows through me with ease.
I walk this earth with reverence.
                    Sizzling.
                        Engaging.
                            Loving.
                                Endless.
                                    Nurturing.
                                        Abundant.
Thank you, God.
I am achieving.   I am contributing.
I am filled with grace.   I am possibility focused.
I am worthy of greater and greater good.
I am kind, and my world responds in kind.
Amen. Surely. Verily. Truly.

Eagerness. Talent. Freedom.

My friend's enthusiasm is palpable.
She radiates a *joie de vivre* that is inimitable.

Kat is a powerhouse.

Life Force! Creative Spirit! Divine Mind!
Thank you!
You are the Source of all that is.
I am ONE with You, and I am madly in love with myself!
Love makes the world go around.
Love is my fuel!
When I show up, I light up the room with Your Spirit.
My style is buoyant.
I stand out wherever I am.
I am creative, ingenious, and resourceful.
I am an original …
In each moment, I am humming with divine élan.
As I contemplate our sacrosanct union, I know that Divine Life
Energy is who I am.
I am …
    Keen,
        Active,
            Tenacious.

I honor and venerate our conversations. I appreciate Your wisdom.
I realize that with You all things are possible.
I persevere in my endeavors to be closer to You, and as I do, I am
closer with those around me.
I am a friend.
I celebrate the happiness that permeates all aspects of my existence.
My curiosity is another gift that adds opulence and magnificence to
all that I do.
I am so excited.
My zeal is my imprint.
Thank you!
Thank you!
Thank you!
I appreciate the multiple dimensions of my dazzling life's gem.
I know this is who I am. Love. Joy. And so much more.
I am blessed.

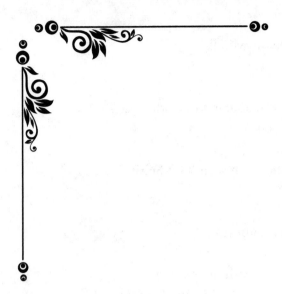

Some people reflect sanctity as they intercede for others.

I see Mary as a restoring presence.

I am One with Divine Mind.

I am One with all that is.

There is a joy in me that comes with my connection with You, dear God.

The Christ Spirit within is my Source of true joy.

The joy of Spirit is an eternal flame.

It lights my way back home to love, understanding, and well-being.

In the presence of Christ joy, I am encouraged.

I am aware of the goodness, love, peace, and strength that are in each of us and in our world.

In prayer today, and every day, I know true joy, the unquenchable joy of Spirit.

I am devoted to learning and discovering the Truths that inspire.

I believe in the daily miracles that stimulate my faith.

I believe in the abundance of the Universe.

I believe that when I give up resistance to my good, my good flows through me in ease.

I believe in the curative sovereignty of forgiveness.

I believe in surrendering to my dreams.

I am **Miraculous**.

I am **Aware**.

I am **Rare**.

I am **Yielding**.

So it is that in this moment I renew my ongoing pledge to accepting my sanctity in whole.

Wherever I am, I am centered in my sacredness.

I reach out to others and affirm our mutual extensions of our holiness.

Life is to be lived.

I accept my majesty.

I give thanks for my delight.

I give thanks for my pleasures.

I give thanks for all that is yet to be.

A smiling gracefulness.
  A genuine beauty.

Yes. Darlene radiates her joy wherever she is.

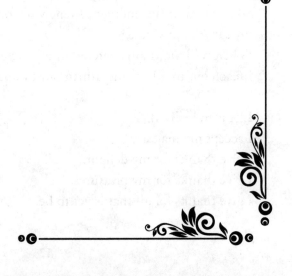

Wow!

What a splendid life!

I am living the dream!

I celebrate my spiritual journey!

I am in my right, perfect place, unfolding my bliss!

How great is that?

Sometimes, in the moment, I might ask, "Why me? Why now?"

And then I remember.

No matter what is in front of me, all is in divine order.

In another moment, I might say, "This is breathtaking, brilliant, beautiful."

And I recall.

No matter what is in front of me, I know that it is all GOOD!

I breathe in the air of courage.

Filled with the power that was present at Jericho, I triumph.

   Any wall keeping me from my success comes tumbling down.

I am a radiating center of Divine love attracting my good. I radiate good to others.

This joyful, love-filled, victorious life is my inheritance.

I revel in the glory of my expression.

> Discerning wisdom …
> Authentic compassion …
> Remarkable clarity …
> Luminous countenance …
> Enlightening energy …
> Nourishing acceptance …
> Exquisite beauty …

I humbly accept the magnanimous nature of my world.

Wow!

I am ever so grateful.

I am dream focused.

To teach. To serve. To renew.

When I am with my friend, Linda, I feel her divine essence reaching out to me.

I appreciate her boundless compassion.

Meeting other Linda's is a genuine gift.

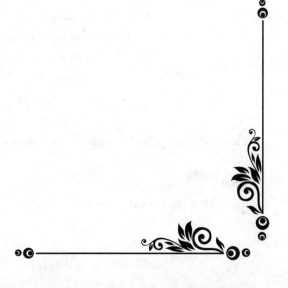

My Paradise is here and now.

Divine Mind, the Energy of Creation, lives in me.

I go within, and I am at peace.

With each passing day, I grow more and more.

I remember: "Things are only impossible—until they're not."

When I think of the immensity of the cosmos, I am filled with wonderment at my place in it.

I am made of stardust.

I am a supernatural creation.

I am an expanding being. I have no beginning and no end.

My soul throbs with amazement and curiosity.

I know every cell in my body reverberates with good health.

I know I am ageless.

I know I am on a course that's zig-zagging toward greater spiritual mastery.

My holiness shines through all that I do.

I cheer and celebrate with every beat of my heart.

I am intentionally joyful.

I am ...

    Limitless.

        Immortal.

            Nurturing.

                Divine.

                    Activating.

On this voyage across space and time, my fellow pilgrims and I rejoice and prosper.

We use contrast to affirm and bring to fruition that which we really want.

We are faith-filled, powerful, eager, and visionary.

I am grateful for the shared learnings.

I am wise.

I am in harmony with the formless pool that holds all manifestation.

I am loving.

I am blessed.

Yes! I am!!!

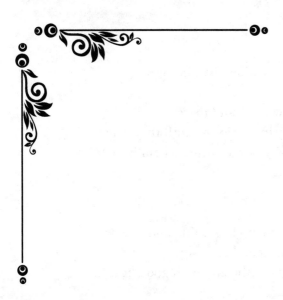

It was a metaphysics class.
    What a gathering.

So much sharing, learning, and querying.

I discovered so much.

Dear Heavenly Spirit,

Thank you!   Thank you!   Thank you!
I arrived here on this plane directly from Source Energy.
It was dramatic! It has been awe-inspiring.
Coming from Divine Energy smack dab into a physical state that
wants to protect me by being über vigilant and cautious brings many
opportunities to remember Who I am.
I chose this journey. It has been magnificent.
I am filled with Joy!
Every day, I find many, many reasons to be grateful—to be in a state
of grace.
I know that I am the reflection of the world of me and my brethren.
I know that I am ONE with all that is—that we are all ONE.
I know that my thoughts create my results.
I know that I am Infinite Spirit in this material vessel, and I am
immortal.
And with each passing tick of the clock, I grow ever closer to
expressing my Divine Essence more and more.
I make progress. I continue to learn.
Most recently, I have been in class with other glorious souls.
This has been a great gift! They have traveled their individual paths to
be here in Time.
I am grateful for their sharing. We are a generous bunch with
unconditional acceptance of each other.
This is the life! Giving up judgments. Giving up pretense. Giving up
having to be right.
We come together bringing our vulnerabilities and authenticity.
We celebrate each other and with our curiosity explore deeper Truths.
We are spiritual virtuosos bringing our many talents and our genius.
We bring Sacredness, Understanding, Divine Spark, Adoration,
Nobility, Blessings, Universal Spirit, Fulfillment, Flourishing States of
Being, Imagination, and Evocative Power.

We are sensational, unique, eternal, sizzling, engaging, loving, endless, nurturing, abundant, keen, active, tenacious, miraculous, aware, rare, yielding, discerning, authentic, remarkable, luminous, enlightening, nourishing, exquisite, limitless, immortal, nurturing, divine and activating.

Thank you! I am ready!
I welcome each moment with an open heart, open mind, and open arms!
I chill out! I tune in! I bask in the glory of me—of You—of my fellow "godlings."
I release, and I let go! I am in the flow!

Your beloved,
Me

Shades! Paints! Colors!

Everywhere I turn, I am struck by hues so rich they vibrate.

I met someone who makes a living selling her artwork.
Melinda dresses in living color, and her work is dyed to match.

The beauty of the morning sky is stunning—
a canvas of peach, azure, lavender, and wisps of mauve.
It drapes itself over my majestic landscape, embracing treetops of
evergreen tinged with malachite and a full spectrum of hues of green.
These are the colors of life—the colors of my life.

The mountain reaches upward, swathed in shades of white, gray, and
ecru.
The road stretches ahead, unfurling in shades of silver and steel.
The fields are dotted with carmine, daffodil, and lavender.
These are the colors of the earth—the colors of my earth.

Amaranth, Bisque, Cerulean, Denim, Emerald, Fuchsia, Ginger,
Harlequin, Iris, Jonquil, Kiwi, Lust, Mahogany, Navy, Onyx,
Periwinkle, Quartz, Razzmatazz, Scarlet, Turquoise, Umber,
Verdigris, Wisteria, Xanadu, Yellow, Zaffre. Life's color palette is
infinite, breathtaking, thrilling.

This startling splendor reminds me of more of life's miracles.
    The birds singing.
        The ants scurrying.
            The bees sipping.
                The squirrels hurrying.
                    The worms scrunching.
                        The butterflies flurrying.

I am a sibling of all of life's creations.
I am a shimmering rainbow of creativity honoring life in all of its
expressions.
I manifest abundance in thought and in deed.

As I am steeped in a pool of magnificence, I affirm …
  The works of art I create are **M**ajestic.
  I step into each day with **E**xpectancy and faith.
  I **L**avish the world with my passion.
  I am **I**ncandescent in my expression.
  I transform my **N**ascent desires into reality.
  I accept the **D**ivinity that flows through me.
  I am **A**udacious, and I flourish.

The Universe is boundless, and the colors of my being scintillate.

Have you ever met someone who is so vigorous and chooses to be someone's shadow?

Lara is powerful in her own right.
I know she realizes her majesty.
She invests all her doing and energy in support of her hubby's endeavors.

What affection! What empowerment!

As I glimpse the morn's first light, the unlimited potential of the day
dazzles my senses.
I know that bubbles of joy await.

A child's giggle.
A robin's song.
A feline's purr.
A butterfly's whisper.

My soul delights in these marvels.
All of nature abounds with the fruits of the Universe.

I look up and around and I see more magic.

An azure dome.
A luminous orb.
A floating cloud.
An open-armed pine.
A winged flock.

In these moments of connecting with the majesty of Creation,
I realize that just like the moon and the stars,
I am a splendid thing.

I am talented, awe-inspiring, and brilliant.
As I step into the world as the "me" that I adore. I am bold. I dare.

 I am Loving every breath I take, every friend I make.
 I am Active—living with verve and enthusiasm.
 I am Resourceful, ingenious, clever, creative, and MORE!
 I am Audacious. And I love it!

I am grateful for the divine spark of being.

I accept my majesty.
I revel in my creativity.
I anticipate my good.
I manifest abundance.

For I am a splendid thing.

In Greek, the meaning of the name Galyn is tranquil.

What a spot-on name.

Galyn thrives on her writing, her teaching, and her Tarot card readings.
She is soothing, calm, gentle.

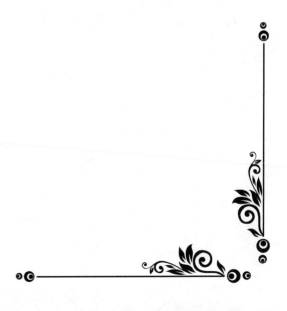

A caterpillar, a chrysalis, a butterfly ...
A seed, a seedling, a flower ...
A log, a match, a fire ...

I look around, and I see the magic of one substance developing into a new manifestation.

Energy turns into matter ...
Water transforms into steam ...
Electricity becomes light ...

All of life is a mystery, a never-ending circle of potential.
I am one with that ring of possibility.
I am of the same cosmic dust that spawned our universe.

I see that each moment is ripe with the germ of what is.

I am imbued with the energy of transmutation, and I choose to play in this sphere.
I believe that my every action alters my world.

I change one substance into another.
I change one form into another.
I change one nature into another.

When I teach, I plant ideas that transform the lives of my students.
When I write, I alter the fabric of consciousness on the planet.
When I serve, I live large, and others see their divinity.

I am **G**enius in motion.
  I inspire **A**we in how I express.
    I impart **L**uminosity.
      I am like a "**Y**erba sagrada"—a holy balm. I heal.
        I **N**urture, and I enliven.

When I create, I am a channel for Universal energy.
  When I connect, I am fulfilled.
    When I live in my spirituality, I am truly bigger than my
    reality.

        I am manifesting abundance.
          I am an alchemist.
            I am divine.

Carol. Carol. Carol.

What a coincidence that the word carol can connote song, hymn, and chant.

Carol is a magnificent cello player.

She devotes her free time to nurturing plants and growing community.
    She is a supreme gift.

Spiders weave the fabric of their soul.
　　Fireflies shimmer in their unique glow.
　　　　Ants work for community growth.

　　　　　I see the tiniest creatures diligently living a grand design.

Birds sing their spirit's cry.
　　Dogs frolic in excitement, jumping high.
　　　　Fish swim their days in love with their lives.

　　　　　I am inspired by the purposefulness of these mighty spirits.

Stars light the canopy of the night sky.
　　The sun nurtures all of earth's plant life.
　　　　The moon peers down and brightens with light.

　　　　　I am affirmed by the life-giving intention of our Universe's
　　　　　　　　　　　　　　　　　　　majestic mosaics.

As I contemplate the mysteries of existence on this plane,
　　I know that I too have a purpose.

My life has meaning.

When I listen to my heart's desires, I know I am potential personified.
When I respond to that inner urging and deliver on the chit of gifts I
have within,

　　　　　　　　　　　　　　　　　　　　　　I sparkle.
And so it is that I acknowledge my gifts, my power, and I am strong.
I manifest abundance.

I **C**oach others and magnify each person's being.
I express my talents, and I attract **A**ffluence.
I am **R**adiant in my relationships, and life is in love with me.
My **O**ptimism is contagious, and the world is lighter.
I live a life that **L**ifts me to my highest good, and I thrive.

I am living the meaning of me.
I am kinship.
I am peace.
I am.

I love learning.
    I love learners.
I love those who dare to keep growing.

Thank you, Martin.
I appreciate your role as a way-shower.

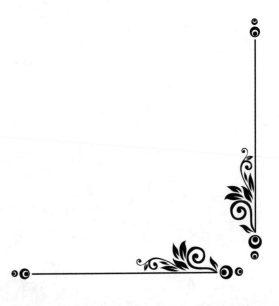

As I've journeyed on this blue bus suspended in the sky,
I've realized that I love to learn and teach.

There is an urge blazing inside of me, propelling me to synthesize new
expressions.
I love that I am a channel of understanding so that others birth
ideas.

Knowledge is the music of the Universe.
It rings throughout all of Creation.

It is why
… a spider knows how to weave a web that sustains;
a bird knows how to form a nest that nurtures;
geese know how to fly in formation and relieve;
bees know how to manufacture a hive for honey;
beavers know how to take those logs and build a dam.

I anticipate opportunities for new manifestation.
Maybe it's the quest, a sense of exploration, perhaps an exciting activity
that transform me into a magician.
I conjure up new structures of comprehension.

I appreciate and lovingly accept my gifts …

Mastery of learning.
   Adventure in living.
      Rapture in being.
         Thankfulness for loving.
            Inspiration in edifying.
            Navigator in choosing.

I love that I feel that Universal knowledge pulsing in
every cell in my body.
It is tenacious in wanting to grow.
It is unrelenting in wanting to be shared.
I was born to synthesize.
I was born to teach.

I manifest abundance at every turn.

A caregiver.
A teacher of toddlers.
A matchless family support.
This is Candasa.

One plus two is three.
Basic, right?

Well, there are times when, truly, the whole is greater than the sum of its parts.
When one plus two *is* greater than three.

Take my family ...
My sweetie and I are definitely experiencing an intimate connection.
It seems that we flow into each other's being effortlessly.
And as another family member joins us,
I feel the sharing and feeling at one with each other expand.

Now instead of one to one, it can be two to one, the three together, a different one to one, many possibilities.
This is magic.
Truly a miracle.

I have gotten back in touch with what it means to have this deep relationship.
I am reminded that it's not about me; it's about "we."
I am reminded that as we get closer, we deepen our mutual understanding and regard.
As we continue to connect, to share our interests, our bond to the divine seems to intensify.

When I look out into the world, I see the Universe is filled with the enchantment of community.

A flock of geese flying south for the winter.

A new litter of pups discovering mom and each other.

A colony of ants carrying food home for the group.

In every moment, I am grateful for these gifts ...

The **C**ommunity we **co**-create.

Abundance in love, support, and joy.

The **N**ascent dimension of our love blooming.

The **D**iscovery of souls linking up in holiness.

The **A**ffection that fills my moments.

The **S**anctuary of my family.

The **A**ppreciation that comes my way, every day.

I am blessed.

The light in me sees the light in you.

Namasté.

I am the creator of my own life.

A dog lover …
　　A business aficionado …
　　　A community devotee …

John laughs, and the world laughs with him.
I appreciate the effervescence he shares.

I see a hummingbird making friends with a flower,
and I see giving and receiving.
I see a father gazing into his baby's eyes, and the
love flows unconditionally.
My beloved is listening to my heart's desires, and I am transformed.

Giving and receiving.

The moon dances with the tides, and creation goes on.
The sun caresses the leaves on the tree, and life is exchanged.
My dog leans into me, and mutual understanding springs to life.

Giving and receiving.

The rhythm of life is constantly flowing through my moments.

I love the joyful connections that serendipitously bless me.
At times, there is pain. And what I call a mistake
is God's way of making miracles happen.
I'm in love with life.

I appreciate the serenity as much as the hustle-bustle.
Laughter fills my amusement cells.
The grandeur of the forest amplifies my being.
The eagle watching over my house fills me with wonder.

Giving and receiving.

Quantum mechanics postulates that there are eleven dimensions.
Universes upon universes.
Higgs Boson, the God particle, materializing from nothing.
Miracles begetting miracles.

Giving and receiving.

I am **J**uvenescent.
I am **O**ptimistic.
I am **H**opeful.
I am **N**oble.

I am open and receiving.

I am open and accepting life.

Libby's mom was undergoing treatment for a severe ailment.

We shared some special moments.
What encouragement.
I am grateful.

The ebb and flow of the ocean waters on the shore …

The light of day and the darkness of night …

The yin of the feminine and the yang of the masculine …

The bright side of life and the shadow of the soul …

This is the mystery that propels the Universe to manifestation.

It is a dynamic where one does not exist without the other.
They appear to be separate in nature when in fact they are part of the whole.
This is a sacred dance: riding the waves of life to create balance, to give life to harmony.

I sit here contemplating the stages of our existence on this plane.

We are born of Spirit onto this planet in this Universe.
As we progress from decade to decade, our physical being metamorphosizes.
That baby that was in my mother's womb is also the person I am now.
Yet we are not the same.
I am not the teenager that explored this world with zeal and curiosity.
Yet that zeal and curiosity live on in me.

So I am struck by the changes in my mother.
I realize that impermanence is a basic phenomenon.
Still—I am shaken by the threat on her existence by a life-altering illness.

How do I ride this chaotic wave?

How do I navigate this new territory?

How do I synchronize that internal tug-of-war, of holding on and releasing?

How do I honor the turbulent emotions rising within me and balance my external harmony with those closest to me?

The yin and yang symbol is known also as the symbol of 'tai chi'— the Chinese word that literally means *ultimate potentiality.*

Ultimate potentiality. I love it. Why do I continue to buy into the premise that what we have here on earth is the ultimate potentiality? Life and Death. Yin and Yang.

I am ...

    Lithe,   **Immortal,**   **Blissful,**   **Brave,**   **Yielding.**

I am One with all Life.

Courage. Daring. Discovery.

Loretta manifests these talents and easily imparts to others as they unfold.

As a counselor, she empowers.

I read the other day that the trajectory of an Apollo rocket is actually on course only 2 or 3 percent of the time. At least 97 percent of the time it takes to get from the earth to the moon, it's off course. Put another way, for every half hour the ship is in flight, it is on course for less than sixty seconds. Another source said it was on course 7 percent of the time. In either case, that's quite a phenomenon.

How it makes it to the moon is pretty fantastic. The earth is rotating and revolving on its axis.
The starry sea presents unknown challenges. The moon isn't simply sitting still.

Kind of reminds me of life.
My intention sets the course. And people around me flex. Conditions change.
The decisions of others can alter my plans.
I can make different, more informed choices.
I gain clarity and have a destination in mind as I keep checking if I am on course.

Fundamentally, I believe that alignment is a process.
I love the idea that this Universe was spun to life from chaos.

An experiment with pendulums found that the pendulums, when pushed by forces according to a regular rhythm, behaved chaotically and swung out of sync. Yet when the researchers introduced disorder, applying forces at random intervals to each oscillator, they began to swing in synch. The "forces" were applied along the rods of the "pendulums" to make them swing. Order from chaos.

I accept these gifts …
Love—feelings of tender affection and compassion.
Opportunity—a combination of favorable circumstances or situations.
Reverence—feelings of deep respect or devotion.
Enlightenment—achievement of the realization of a spiritual understanding or self-awareness.
Transformation—conversion of one form of energy to another.
Triumph—that feeling of happiness/pride that comes from being victorious, overcoming something.
Ability—having the necessary skill or talent to do that which is important.

I was built to believe.

I was designed to receive.

I was born to discover my greatness with every choice I make.

I am joyfully aligned with my divine self.

Heroes all around.

They love and sometimes grieve.

My friend Lynn's vulnerability strengthened me.

Souls meeting souls.

Hearts embracing hearts.

Love stirring love.

This is the stuff of miracles.

My bird passed away recently, and I was in despair.
I was reminded that life is not the privilege of just us humans.
I was reminded that this body suit I wear is not who I am.
I am the divine essence of all that is.
And so is every other living creature.

What about birds?

Some think that humankind is at the top of the evolutionary chain.
Really?
Birds evolved from dinosaurs around 160 million years ago.
They survived the dinosaur extinction sixty million years ago.
They are survivors. They pre-date humans. They are our planetary
ancestors.

Birds are the masters of flight. Human beings had to invent airplanes.
Many social species exhibit cultural transmission of knowledge across
generations.

There are so many types of birds, around ten thousand living species.
Small ones. Large ones. Colorful ones. Talkative ones. Mellifluous
ones.

Aren't they amazing?

Beyond all these impressive facts about these animals,
even more impressive is their ability to meet us in the realm of our
sacred-ness.

They come into our lives and show us the true meaning of
"unconditional acceptance."

The language of unconditional love is primal. It is the original seed of
life.
The animals we invite into our lives and those that find us bring us
true gifts.
They are the magi of our being.

Luminosity in the radiance of holy spirits meeting on this plane,
    Yielding to the beauty of spiritual connection,
        Nurturing universal unfoldment, and
            Nourishing that fire that is the light in each of us.

This is who I am.

The hero of my hero's journey.

Alicia is unique, vibrant, exploring.

Her intimate reflection on her personal meaning made a difference.

Walking through the forest, I spotted some sturdy, stunning alder trees.
Each one was different, unique. Each one had its own charm.
Then a couple of friendly squirrels were scrutinizing me from atop a rock.
One was gray and chubby, while the other was tan in color and sleek.
A bit further in, I came across an expanse of wildflowers.
Oh my! What a sight! Beautiful and in so many colors and sizes!

We live in a universe of inimitable creations.
Not only that—we live in a universe that is forever inventing out of experimentation.
The story of evolution tells us that.
Humans developed in small increments that accumulated to bring about significant change.

So, what is this telling me?
There is no one else like me!
And my life's experiments are glorious.
Even the ones I call failures,
    for they are bringing about that significant change of the
    immortals.

It's telling me I'm okay just as I am.
Heck—I'm more than okay!
I am creating this ME with enthusiasm.

I ask myself, "Why are there so many songs about self-acceptance?"
Is it because we get into the habit of judgments?
Of ourselves and others?

There is a song about living life my way.
For me, it's about having the image I project be as true as possible.
I know that I am who I'm meant to be. I am divine expression and
God's manifestation of life!
I am …
Ardent, **L**ovely, **I**nfinite, **C**ourageous, **I**ncandescent, **A**uthentic.

I am an adventurous, infinite being, enjoying the shared joy of wildly
creative expression.

Joy!

 Miracles!

  Power!

   Divinity!

Linda has been a Religious Science Practitioner for decades.

I see the magnificence of the stars in their heavenly lair
    … the splendor of a rainbow in the sky.
I smell the life-giving freshness of the morning air
    … the miracle of each day passing by.

Yes! I am One with this amazing Universe.

The pitter-patter of the rain …
    The joyful chirping of the birds …
        The rushing murmur of an ocean wave …
            The empowering energy of love's words …

Yes! I am One with this wondrous Universe.

> I find joy in supporting others.
> I find joy in my millinery creativity.
> I find joy in my sisters and brothers.
> I find joy in life's festivity.
>
> I am divinity expressing.

When I pray with another, the eternal Truth unfolds.
When I'm with my family, I am truly a blessing to behold.

Yes! I am One with this marvelous Universe.

As I gaze into the warmth in my pet's eyes. I am soothed.
As I gaze into the woods. I am inspired.
When I touch my sweetheart, I am cherished. **L**
    When I laugh with a friend, I am sanctified. **I**

                                                         N

Yes! I am One with this stunning Universe. **D**

                                                          A

Just like the Universe, this is who I am!
        Amazing!   Wondrous!   Marvelous!   Stunning!

Just like the one on this blue boat (earth) in the galaxy, this is who
I am!
      Loving!   **Inspiring!**   **Nurturing!**   **Discerning!**   **Alive!**

She's been an executive.

She stokes others' abilities.

Marsha's extended family was in a Japanese internment camp.

I am thankful her compassion lifts all of us.
She provides scholarships to disadvantaged youth.
We all benefit.

The rains are soothing, emboldening the globe …
    The sun smiles upon the earth, promoting creation …
        The winds carry seeds of newness, fostering fresh growth …

The Universe! … facilitating immeasurable expansion for the cosmos!

A dog nurtures her new litter, bestowing unconditional love …
    A bird feeds her young in the nest, invigorating the sacred circle of
        life …
        An ant carries food to the colony, nourishing the village …

Yes, each—one singular life form—affirming the spirit!

Loving strangers supporting people living in the street.
    Teachers urging their students to experiment and learn.
        Volunteers helping out at a hospital.

This connection is a reflection of the one-ness of all that is.
We are here for each other.

I've been fortunate to have had a life filled with amazing, encouraging
people.
People who have opened portals of opportunity through which I
could stride.
People who were examples of leadership and ingenuity.

Of course, I knew I had specific, important talents.
    And I had aspirations.
Sometimes they believed in me—often more than I did.
What gifts!

One friend especially stands out. She facilitated many paths.

There was:
    Meaningful contribution,
        Authentic consideration,
            Radiant empathy,
                Significant discernment,
                    Healthy backing,
                        Abundant collaboration.

All a divine offering—glorious, helpful, insightful.

I am blessed by being in the flow of love and contribution.
    I am open to reciprocating to others.
        I am grateful for my friend.

A technocrat. An artist. A writer.

So many gifts!
Keith shares so effortlessly and generously.

I love his writing classes. He's the best.

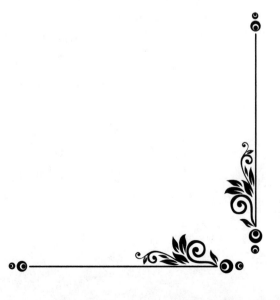

A child bouncing on the trampoline ever higher!
    What zest! What delight!

A hot-air balloon transporting one to the sky!
    What openness! What curiosity!

A dancer unfettering of time and space!
    What abandon! What rapture!

I get a glimpse of that field of infinite potential.
    A glimpse of the energy that is the basic building block of galaxies.
    A glimpse of that personal journey of inspiration and the
relinquishment of the predictable.

The panorama surrounding us is boundless.
The sky, the land, and the water here on this blue dot I call earth are
microscopic in comparison.
Wow! What power. What possibility. What promise.

We are born into a Supreme Creative Playground.
Every present moment is a doorway to a new future.
I am not surprised when I meet beings who transcend present milieus.
    Wizards. Sorcerers. Sorceresses. Shamans. Magicians.

These geniuses of originality bubble over with endowments, aptitudes,
and flairs in …
    Art. Science. Song. Sculpting. Dance. Writing.

So many talents. So many ways of expressing the divine intelligence propelling nature.

So many opportunities to craft stellar masterpieces.

And, like genies, these souls encourage other human hearts and animate bottled-up treasures.

They support others in creating something remarkable, exceptional.

They sometimes edify in small, sparse spaces—community centers.

An author on memoirs asserts, when transforming memories into stories,

"Be prepared for the revelation of things you don't even dream."

I am this mentor. I dare others to go beyond what they think they can do.

I am a Language Wizard, a Word Artisan, an Encourager of the Heart—a writing don.

Keen and **K**ind.

Effervescent and **E**vocative.

Inventive and **I**ntuitive.

Tenacious and **T**rusting.

Humorous and **H**elpful.

I am magic.

I am inspiration.

I am compassion.

I am.